Life

in

Balance

RealFaithRealLifeseries

This exciting new Bible study series is for men and women in their twenties and thirties who would like to explore relevant issues from a biblical perspective. Each four- to six-session study is theme-based and written from the Reformed tradition. Designed for small, flexible group meetings in nontraditional Christian education settings, these studies are developed to help enrich the faith lives of young adults.

Other Volumes in This Series

Wake Up and Live Your Life!

Future Themes

Faith and Finances

Change: Responding to God's Call

Hypocrites in the Church

Approaching the Bible in Different Ways

To find out more about this series, please call 1-800-524-2612 or visit our Web sites at www.bridgeresources.org or youngadult.pcusa.org.

Life
in
Balance

Page L. D. Creach

Bridge Resources
Louisville, Kentucky

Edited by Rodger Nishioka and David M. Dobson

Book and cover design by Kim Wohlenhaus

First edition

Published by Bridge Resources
Louisville, Kentucky

Web site address: http://www.bridgeresources.org

PRINTED IN THE UNITED STATES OF AMERICA
00 01 02 03 04 05 06 07 08 09 — 10 9 8 7 6 5 4 3 2 1

Library of Congress Cataloging-in-Publication Data
Creach, Page L. D. (Page Leigh Davis), date.
   Real Faith, real life: Life in balance / Page L. D. Creach. — 1st ed.
      p.   cm.
   Includes bibliographical references.
   ISBN 1-57895-077-5
   1. Church group work with young adults. 2. Bible—Study and teaching—
Reformed Church. 3. Young adults—Religious life. I. Title. II. Series.
BV4446.C74 2000
248.8'4—dc21   99-059483

Contents

Letter from the Editors

Greetings! Welcome to Real Faith, Real Life, a series of Bible studies for young adults in their twenties and thirties. These four- to six-session studies are theme-based and written from the Reformed tradition.

These studies are best suited to a small group meeting in a comfortable space, such as someone's house, apartment, or a favorite coffee shop. A group should be no more than twelve persons—eight would be ideal. It is important that participants commit to attending all the sessions, if at all possible. This is crucial for building a level of trust in the group. Each session or meeting should last two hours, with perhaps some additional time before or after for a meal or more social time.

Each participant will need his or her own copy of this study. There is space throughout to take notes, answer questions, or record feelings.

At the first meeting someone should be designated to be the leader for the duration of the course, or you may decide to have a different person lead each session. Either way, this person will function more as a facilitator of discussions and timekeeper of activities than as a lecturer. There will occasionally be instructions for the session leader.

The introduction and biblical reflection sections are crucial for each session. You may decide that each participant should read these before gathering, or you may read these aloud as a group when you meet.

We would like to suggest that you open and close each session with prayer and sharing. Give all persons the chance to lead prayer if they feel comfortable doing so. Also set aside time at the beginning or end for participants to share some of what has been happening in their lives since the group last met. An easy way of doing this is to go around the group and share the highlights and lowlights of their week.

Some of the session designs include a specific way to do sharing and/or prayer. For those that don't, be sure to include this in your time together.

If the four, five, or six sessions are not enough time for your group, consider meeting an extra time or two. Use the first meeting as a time to share a meal, get to know one another, and set the schedule for the coming weeks. You might also use this as a time to assign a leader or leaders and talk about common expectations of participants (e.g., read the background material before each class; pray for one another regularly during the weeks ahead; keep what is shared in the group confidential; etc.).

As Christians, we believe that the Bible is an extraordinary gift from God and therefore the most important book we will ever read or study. Yet studying the Bible is no easy task. Consider having some other resources around as you engage in your study. The list of resources in For Further Study and the Bibliography provide some excellent reference books that may help you.

There are many people who should be recognized for their role in this series, but perhaps none more so than the incredible young adults who took us up on our invitation to help create a usable, meaningful Bible study for men and women in their twenties and thirties. For four days and three nights they resisted the temptations of Santa Fe during Fiesta to focus on the task at hand. They poured their energy, their creativity, their spirit, and their faith into this endeavor, and for that we are most grateful. You may recognize their names, because some of them have become the writers for this series: The Rev. Heather Christensen; The Rev. Page Creach; Christine Gannon; Rachel Hong; Jody Schultz; The Rev. Elizabeth Kaznak Trexler.

Rodger Nishioka
Coordinator, Youth and
Young Adult Ministries

David M. Dobson
Senior Editor, Bridge Resources

Introduction

> One of the scribes came near and heard them disputing with one
> another, and seeing that he answered them well, he asked him, "Which
> commandment is the first of all?" Jesus answered, "The first is, 'Hear, O
> Israel: the Lord our God, the Lord is one; you shall love the Lord your
> God with all your heart, and with all your soul, and with all your mind,
> and with all your strength.' "
>
> —Mark 12:28–30

One of today's most common words of advice is "Get a life!" but finding
one that is lived well is not easy. One reason is that we are complex
human beings living in a world of boundaries with boundless possibilities.
Being earthbound yet heavenly minded, we are created to observe some
limits and at the same time reach for our greatest human potential.
Living between these two ends of the spectrum, with choices everywhere
in between, is our constant struggle.

On the one hand we are the creatures with dominion over the earth;
thus we have the world to keep. It is a multitask, multidirectional,
high-tech age where accuracy and efficiency are everything. And when
we look up from the work we see there are family members waiting for
our love. We look the other way and there are coworkers, neighbors,
communities, church members, and friends to cherish. On the other
hand, we have the rose we long to stop and smell and a personal life—
a body, a mind, and a spirit—to keep.

> Then God said, "Let us make humankind in our image, according
> to our likeness; and let them have dominion over the fish of the
> sea, and over the birds of the air, and over the cattle, and over all
> the wild animals of the earth, and over every creeping thing that
> creeps upon the earth."
>
> (Gen. 1:26)

Our experience is that life lived in any extreme is painful. Days full
of frenzy make life wearisome and give us no peace, and days that
neglect what needs attention bring us loss and a sense of regret. Thus
finding life's balance and holding onto it is our longing.

Someone said people do not like airports because they are a place of rush and confusion. We don't know where we are or how far we have to go by a certain time. There are endless corridors, and everybody is pulling a load and running, or dragging themselves along trying to keep up with the fast pace. In every direction are "hellos" and "good-byes" and endless emotion. Things are beginning or ending all the time. It all culminates in an overwhelming and exhausting venture.

We know life needs balance. We feel it intensely. Our work needs rest; our times of contemplation need times of activity; our physical self needs exercise, and our spiritual self needs care. Undeniably our health is measured by both inner and outer wellness, and our self-emptying requires refilling. Whenever they are either overextended or neglected, the balance wants to be restored.

Therein lies the challenge.

Often we lack the wisdom of knowing when to begin and when to end. We lack the courage to know when to let go and when to accept something as it is. There are many voices that ask us to choose continually between life and death, but there is only one that creates our life and gives it to us. When God is not at the center of everything, directing all our priorities, things will easily be out of balance, and it will seem like life is no longer ours to run; it is running us instead.

When life begins to feel this way, we begin the search for balance. We do not want to be pushed and pulled through all our days. We want to sense the presence of God with us always, keeping us calm, guiding us through every demand and all temptations.

This is an invitation to live life under the lordship of God. It is based on the understanding that as human beings we are created to please only one God, rather than the many other would-be rulers of our lives. Jesus lived by this rule and prayed daily to be thoroughly rooted in God alone. From him we learn this way of consistently arranging our life and centering ourselves in God's peace.

This kind of security and freedom requires our constant awareness of to whom we belong.

The source for these six sessions then is the daily prayer of Jesus, the Shema: "The LORD is our God, the LORD alone. You shall love the LORD your God with all your heart, and with all your soul, and with all your might" (Deut. 6:4–5). In the Gospel of Mark the phrase "and with all your mind" is added to the prayer as Jesus gives it in answer to the scribe who asks, "Which commandment [of the many I have to live by] is the first of all?" (Mark 12:28). The simple answer is unexpected. It cuts through hundreds of confusing laws. It lightens the load that causes so many such great burden. Thus the prayer that summarizes all that matters is often called "the great commandment." To this day, both Christianity and Judaism revere the prayer.

For us, Jesus' answer reveals our Lord's understanding of what we need to survive as we try to stand as we do: between heaven and earth, in spirit and flesh, choosing every day all the things we do, adding or taking away from our life.

These six sessions are written to address the heart of our existence. It is not an attempt to reduce Christian life to a self-help instructional manual with a guarantee for whoever adheres to it to find the good life. It is to know and believe that it all belongs to God. The heart, with its passion and its will; the soul, that holds our longings, our emotions, and our desires; the mind, that reasons and discerns; and the body, that house we live in that gives us our means to move in our world and relate to others.

These were the foundational words for Jesus. They anchored and managed his life from childhood through death. Reciting the command often was Jesus' way of keeping his path always clear, his spirit never divided, and his life well preserved and at the same time well spent. The hope is that this study will help us live with all the tensions and center our divided selves in God—that we might live sanely and richly.

The Structure of a Balanced Life

Scripture: Mark 12:28–30

Introduction

"How shall I get liberation?"

"Find out who has bound you," said the Master.

The disciple returned after a week and said, "No one has bound me."

"Then why ask to be liberated?" said the Master.

That was a moment of Enlightenment for the disciple,

who suddenly became free."[1]

We are in this world juggling life along with everyone else, but as Christians we are encouraged not to be of it—"Do not be conformed to this world, but be transformed by the renewing of your minds, so that you may discern what is the will of God—what is good and acceptable and perfect" (Rom. 12:2). It can all become stressful and laborious. It can all be experienced as a plethora of days written in black ink on a white calendar of continual commitments, but we know it does not have to be like this. There is more to life. If only we could discern the difference between the things that serve God and the things that merely clutter the way. If we could distinguish between what we give that pleases God and what we give that merely piles up inside our hearts until we feel heavy-laden and out of balance. If we could remember that we are created beings called to live our life in every way, we could express it for the praise and glory of God. We work for this. We also rest and play in this. This is the one thing not to forget: We belong to God.

We are welcomed into this way of life through Christ. Jesus always knew what was wise and good. He lived completely, and he lived well. Not that he avoided all pain, suffering, and stress of any kind—far from it. But he chose well. Jesus knew how to serve God and not Caesar. He knew when to do what. He knew how to see greatness in the little things; he understood that holiness is in the ordinary things. He lived and died with great love, and he knew how to abide in God's peace.

1. Robert J. Wicks, *Seeking Perspective: Weaving Spirituality and Psychology in Search of Clarity* (New York: Paulist Press, 1991), p. 24.

Jesus held onto hope, cast out his fear, discerned the proper time, and never ceased in his energy and will to trust God with his whole life.

We strive for a life like his. And when we are weighed down and pulled out of balance, we look all the more to his life for reestablishing our own. We seek his wisdom and his peace. In a demanding world whose power seems able sometimes to swallow us up, we ask again, "How shall we live?"

Christ understood that everything belongs to God as Creator of heaven and earth—the giver, sustainer, and redeemer of all life. This is our worldview too, and it is more than just a few words we learn to recite for church; it is a gift to live by. It becomes ours when we devote every moment, each breath, all relationships, any event, and everything we are to God. When nothing is left outside of the realm of God's guidance and care—not our heart, our mind, our strength, the body, or the soul—we have one source for ordering the chaos of all we have to hold. Understanding this and grounding our lives in this sets us free.

We know God is boundless, and it is our mistake to pretend we are not. When our Lord lived in human form, as spirit and flesh, again and again he stopped to center himself in God. Three times a day he recited the Shema, the prayer he was taught from the Hebrew Scriptures: "Hear, O Israel, the Lord is our God, the Lord alone" (Deut. 6:4). The prayer was his refuge and his strength. It bound up his life with God's rule. It relieved Jesus from a life under the lordship of the culture and freed him from anxiously striving after things that others valued but God did not. Thus it is ours for the same reasons.

In a frenzied world where we feel obligated to so many and so much, these are the words to keep. They gather us around God before we are scattered about, and they balance our life before we are overtaken. They transform us and lead us to what is needful, to what deepens life, not what distracts us from it. The words are given to us for our peace.

Biblical Reflection

"Why is everyone here so happy except me?"

"Because they have learned to see goodness and beauty everywhere," said the Master.

"Why don't I see goodness and beauty everywhere?"

"Because you cannot see outside of you what you fail to see inside."[2]

---

2. Ibid., p. 104.

In Jesus' day, rabbis, scribes, and Pharisees spent a lifetime trying to keep up with over six hundred commandments. Hour after hour they spent in debate. They lived to determine such things as how the obligations of life should be ordered in importance, how they would possibly obey every last command, how they should bind them all on the people, how often any could be broken, and what the penalty would be when they were.

Needless to say, they took all their covenants seriously. They understood things like duty, responsibility, and leadership all too well. To their credit, they were searchers of truth, seekers of the right way and the good life. But they lived rigid lives, lives void of the essential things, like love, and empty of the joyful things, like forgiveness and spontaneity. These were lives that were overwhelmed, since they had 365 commands to remember *not* to do and 248 commands to remember *to* do.

Jesus comes to them in Mark's Gospel with wisdom and help in his hand. When one scribe asks him which commandment should be first, Jesus sweeps them all up into one and gives him something much more manageable. In essence Jesus takes all the human concerns that fill volumes of rule books and cover endless pages of law books and writes one great commandment: "Hear, O Israel, the Lord our God, the Lord is one. You shall love the Lord your God with all your heart, and with all your soul, and with all your mind, and with all your strength" (Mark 12:28–30).

Of course his answer is a great relief for the people heavily burdened with a life of countless demands forced on them. What Jesus offers is a way to totally restructure an individual life—around one idea instead of hundreds. The words Jesus spoke offered freedom to the scribe from the many loyalties boggling his mind and weakening the quality of his life. This way of organizing all things was placed into one daily prayer that seekers had recited every morning, noon, and night since the day they were born. This Shema from Deut. 6:4–5 that Jesus gives the searcher was truly a blessing of simplification. Taking every piece of our human lives, Jesus lays them all down at the feet of God. He puts them all under one motivation: love for God. And then with only one to live for, only one to please and one to obey, an answer regarding much of the chaos of our lives is given. It is a gift of power from a God who is gracious with us. The words serve to remind and define over and over again who God is for the Hebrew people. This is the God who brought Israel out from under Pharaoh, who led them out of Egypt, out of slavery, through the dry desert and the deep sea, into freedom.[3] This is the God who alone should direct our lives. This is the one who can determine best who we should be and what we should or should not do.

To pray the prayer sounds like an easy pledge of allegiance, but to live by the prayer takes a constant dedication to its principle to keep our selves centered in this God of life. The one command is a new challenge for any who dare to pray it sincerely and hope for the goal of becoming single-minded. The call is to test everything by God's pleasure and allow no personal desire or societal pressure to rule any part of you or your days. Instead, the whole person—heart, soul, mind, and bodily strength—is dedicated to God and shaped by God. Notice that this is not a prayer to pray on short notice expecting overnight delivery. This life is not quickly learned or easily accomplished, and the goal of listening for the voice of God alone is done perfectly only by Christ.

Preparation

Those gathered will

- become more aware of the goal of living a life balanced by God
- explore their lifestyles and understand the ways they are fragmented rather than whole
- make conscious choices that will lead them toward living a more balanced life

Key Questions

- Who or what is at the center of your life right now?
- How is your life made heavy to bear because of demands, rules, and obligations?
- What voices rule your life now? How will you begin to listen to God?

Resources Needed

- Bibles
- Name tags
- Newsprint, tape, and marker

---

3. Thomas W. Mann, *Deuteronomy*. Westminster Bible Companion (Louisville: Westminster John Knox Press, 1995), pp. 50–56.

Gathering

Two Truths and a Lie

To the leader: As each participant arrives ask him or her to think of three statements about him- or herself. Two of them should be true and one should be false. For example, "I won a prize in spelling in second grade." "My favorite food is sushi." "I got lost at the zoo when I was little." When the group has gathered, let each person share the three descriptive statements and let the group decide which one is not true. They may hold up one, two, or three fingers to show which statement they think is false. Reveal the answer, and let each person have a turn.

Now ask the participants to draw a face on their name tags that fits how they have felt that day. Then ask them to write their names inside their faces. Allow some time for some casual sharing and "venting" among the group.

Read the following quote from Abraham Heschel. Allow each person to read, reflect, and respond to it:

> Any ideal, human, social, or artistic, if it forms a roof over all of life, shuts us off from the light. Even the palm of one hand may bar the light of the entire sun.[4]

Exploring the Word

Have one person read Deut. 6:4 aloud to the group. Compare translations from the different Bibles each person has brought to the study session. Note any differences you discover. What might they mean?

There are three possible translations for *yhwh 'ehad* from Hebrew into English: (1) "Yahweh is our God, Yahweh alone!"; (2) "Yahweh, our God, is one Yahweh"; (3) "Yahweh is our God, Yahweh is 'One.' "

Write these on newsprint for the group to consider. What difference does the translation make for your understanding?

Biblical scholar Gerhard von Rad suggests the first translation is a confession. Thus, it is a statement of conviction that reinforces our commitment to the God we declare creates, recreates, and rules, not some things, but all things. Remembering helps this affirmation take root in us until we can consciously refuse all other temptations and let no one and nothing else lead, divide, or control our lives.[5]

---

4. As quoted in Wicks, *Seeking Perspective*, p. 10.

5. Gerhard von Rad, *Deuteronomy: A Commentary*. The Old Testament Library (Philadelphia: The Westminster Press, 1966), p. 63.

Life in Balance

The second translation is also a confession, though its emphasis is slightly different. This translation highlights the oneness of Yahweh our God in an effort to distinguish the only God of Israel from the pantheon of other gods in ancient times. In an age where divine beings were believed to have power only over one part of creation or another and varying degrees of influence within this world, Israel had one God who ruled it all.[6]

The third translation suggests that "one" can be a title or a name for our God: God's name is "One." Even here the statement summons us to single-minded living with the one God in whom all things live, move, breathe, find meaning, and find coherence. The key word in all of these translations is a delightful one.[7]

Each of these translations is well supported, and every interpretation calls us to unite ourselves under God's rule, serving one will rather than many. Our hope for greater balance in all our days hangs on this refreshing idea of living to please God alone.

Have one person in the group read aloud Deut. 6:5. Then ask one person to read Mark 12:28 and another to read Mark 12:29–30. Write on newsprint the three ways we are to love God according to Deut. 6:5. Then write down the four ways to love God according to Mark 12:29–30.

Consider how the addition may have occurred and what difference it makes:

- How did Mark expand on the commandment from the book of Deuteronomy? *What difference does it make?*
- What does the word *might* mean to you?
- Do the words *mind* and *strength* change the meaning of the command?
- How does this one command help simplify your life?

When the question of the greatest commandment was put to Jesus, it must have seemed like Jesus was being asked to look down into a bottomless pit and pull out one correct answer. What Jesus said was plain but profound. Of all the laws to be obeyed, prophets' words to follow, and writings to remember, Jesus said simply to love God with all we are. Of course he leaves nothing uncovered in the whole human being's life when he chooses his answer from Deut. 6:5. In the Hebrew

---

6. Ibid., p. 63.

7. Peter C. Craigie, *The Book of Deuteronomy* (Grand Rapids: Wm. B. Eerdman's Publishing Co., 1976), p. 168.

language, the request is for our life to belong to God and our love to be expressed in three ways: with heart, soul, and might (*dunamis* means "power"). This fulfills all life's demands, he assured, and since there is nothing left to withhold, it must.

When the Gospel of Mark was recorded, a different translation from the Hebrew was used. The effect is that Jesus asks for four things to be dedicated to God: the heart, soul, mind (*dianoia*), and strength (*ischus*) instead of "might." The expansion adds nothing more. Both bid us to become more completely given to God. The answer to all the questions about how to live is the same. We dedicate every part of our life and being to God.[8]

In the next four sessions, we will discuss ways to love God with our heart, soul, mind, and strength. The increased awareness that God's glory may be seen in each of these areas of our lives may change the way we face life and live it. We might begin to see new ways to accept or reject all that comes our way. We might discover a better way to live. Perhaps we will gain a new sense of power to make better choices in the way we deal with stress and pain and the way we expend our human strength. And the God of peace and life might rule over our hearts, minds, and bodies more completely.

Living the Word

From the Lord who says, "Come to me, all you that are weary and are carrying heavy burdens, and I will give you rest. Take my yoke upon you, and learn from me; for I am gentle and humble in heart, and you will find rest for your souls" (Matt. 11:28–29), the possibility of restructuring our lives is new for us every day. We can choose today to live by one rule if we can see the freedom that comes from living by the One who gives life and promises more.

Ways to Practice

Listen to a favorite piece of music. Being conscious of God, give yourself completely to the emotional range of the music. Open yourself to the lyrics or the rhythms and the melodies as if they are a devotional you are reading. When the music is finished, breathe a prayer expressing the feelings with which you are in touch.

The next time you are out shopping, walking, or running, let that be a devotional time. As you see people, consciously consider what

8. Morna D. Hooker, *A Commentary on the Gospel According to St. Mark* (London: A&C Black, 1991), p. 287.

Life in Balance

might be behind their faces. What might they be facing; feeling? What is common to us all? Afterward pray a simple prayer for your own peace.

Write out your typical daily schedule.

_____

_____

_____

_____

Reflect on times, places, activities, and people that could call you to remember God. Now mark different places in your day when you will stop to think about God's purpose for your life. Pray and give thanks.[9]
Note to the Leader: If you have time, you may want to use this last practice as a group activity.

Questions

- How will you begin to live differently with the idea of God as your sole ruler?
- If you choose to let only God's voice rule your life, what will the consequences be? What will the rewards be?
- How does understanding God's claim for every part of you change the way you are living?

Closing

Close with prayer, reflecting on the following quote: "Prayer is a yearning for one's true home. Follow its lead."[10]

---

9. Harvey and Lois Seifert, *Liberation of Life: Growth Exercises in Meditation and Action* (Nashville: The Upper Room, 1976), pp. 50–52.

10. Keith McClellan, *Prayer Therapy* (St. Meinrad, IN: Abbey Press, 1990), p. 2.

The Undivided Heart

Scripture: Mark 12:30

Introduction

There is a way that leads to life, Jesus teaches, but the path is less traveled because it is harder, the gate is narrow, and those who ever really find it are few (Matt. 7:14). There is the offer. It is the way that involves deep love, for there is nothing greater or more demanding than love's complete devotion, love's full commitment, and love's total trust. Perhaps this is why Jesus said the greatest commandment begins by asking us to seek to love God with all our heart. The moment we accept the challenge, we begin to find our way into a new strength. We will come to know a quiet security for our life of the kind only God and love can provide. And being heart to heart with God can transform everything we encounter.

In *The Road Less Traveled*, psychiatrist M. Scott Peck says a few things about love that are worth remembering:

- "Anyone who genuinely loves knows the pleasure of loving."
- "Commitment is the foundation, the bedrock of any genuinely loving relationship."
- "Genuine love is a self-replenishing activity."
- "There is a paradox in that love is both selfish and unselfish at the same time."
- "In the case of genuine love the aim is always spiritual growth. In the case of nonlove the aim is always something else."[1]

Real love does ask a lot from us. In order to thrive it requires consistent attention and an intense desire to please and not fail the other. But if the rewards of genuine love are deep pleasure, self-emptying that is at the same time self-replenishment, and spiritual growth, then in accepting the command to love God "with all our heart," we receive good things for life in return.

---

1. M. Scott Peck, *The Road Less Traveled: A New Psychology of Love, Traditional Values, and Spiritual Growth* (New York: Simon & Schuster, 1978), pp. 116, 140.

If we decide to pursue a relationship with the sacred that is wholehearted, we will need to consider how to cultivate one. Of course time will have to be committed to it. One of the points in the Gospel story of Mary, Martha, and Jesus was that while Martha was busy cooking and preparing as a way to express her love for Jesus, Mary was sitting still, listening to him. Jesus loved them both, but when pressed for an answer as to what was most necessary, he said Mary had chosen the thing that was needful (Luke 10:42).

So a heart given to God means we will begin to look for a time to commune regularly with God—to sit, walk, talk, and simply be with God. And while it may be hard to find another minute to share with anybody in our day, the hope of loving God with all your heart will require such discipline and effort. Hopefully, it will not be a chore but a welcome and beneficial daily moment: a breath of fresh air for your soul.

There is great variety in the way the human heart connects with God. It may involve a moment of reflection any place at all; a brief pause for a prayer; or a meditation that calls the whole body, mind, and spirit all into the heart of God who is for us, the only one who holds us in balance. Songs, works of art, times of retreat, worship experiences, and special places can also help to bring us to the heart of God. The choices are rich, but all require a sense of oneness, a way to feel that the presence of God is with you.

If the heart can learn how to belong solely to God, it will become an undivided heart at last. And the experience of living with an undivided heart is priceless in this world. The daily effort to let the whole heart rest in God is what centers and stabilizes the whole self. It will not lead us away from the world; it will guide us into it with new compassion and identification. We will move along under the unseen hand of God's steadfast love, with God's breath in us, and with God's eyes fastened to our heart.

For those who are asking what really matters, how to simplify their life, or what will restore life's balance, the investment it will take to build and nurture the sacred relationship is worth more than the value of our precious time.

Biblical Reflection

"What good work shall I do to be acceptable to God?"

"How should I know?" said the Master. "Your Bible says that

Abraham practiced hospitality and God was with him. Elias loved to pray and God was with him. David ruled a kingdom and God was with him too."

"Is there some way I can find my own allotted work?"

"Yes. Search for the deepest inclination of your heart and follow it."[2]

The heart is a fascinating place to try to describe. Physically, it is the beating of our life from minute to minute. It is an organ central to everything else. It represents all our vitality; our life quite literally flows from its healthy, rhythmic pulse. Psychologically, the heart is that inner part of us that is deepest and most capable of hiding our selves away. It is the house of our truest thoughts, our most honest emotions. Our unmasked and unspoken feelings reside here—those that are noble and those that are not.

It has been suggested that the power of the heart is best described "by the Greek word *enthumesis*, which signifies the act of meditating, conceiving, imagining, projecting, and ardently desiring."[3]

Aristotle also thought about the heart. He noted that the organs that sense the world run to the heart. He saw, for instance, how taste and touch link the heart to the world. Others came behind him and reasoned the same, but they emphasized the priority of the heart. They said that the heart is at work feeling and believing in something before the tongue is moved to speak, or the mind to think, or the body to act. They noticed how the heart is busy forming impressions and perceptions from feelings and images it has received from the outside world and the self's personal experiences in it. And furthermore, they agreed that if the thoughts of the heart are strong, then the tongue will speak with great passion, the mind will think with boldness, and the body will move with all the vigor it can muster.[4]

Jesus wanted all the heart to belong to God. He wanted his own heart to receive its vitality day after day from the inexhaustible, living God. He tells the scribe that the world cannot divide and conquer his body, mind, or spirit if his heart belongs to God. We also hear this good news. We may be downcast or downtrodden, but we are not

---

2. Based on information in *One-Minute Wisdom*, by Anthony De Mello (New York: Doubleday & Company, Inc., 1986).

3. Henry Corbin, as quoted in *The Thought of the Heart and The Soul of the World*, by James Hillman (Dallas: Spring Publications, Inc., 1981), p. 5.

4. Hillman, *The Thought of the Heart*, pp. 11–16.

overtaken and left out of balance if our heart reacts to God's voice alone.

The spiritual writer Evelyn Underhill understood what it means to love God with all your heart. She believed the only way to become fully human was to "be in love with the Absolute" and allow your character to be shaped and changed as a consequence of it. She was convinced that personal confrontation with God was "the most important human experience."

So Underhill practiced having a love for God deep in her heart. She kept the loving relationship in shared experiences—to everything she brought with her an awareness of God. She saw that the love between human and the Divine can be exchanged in worship, work, nature, beauty, acts of goodness—even in pain, sickness, and sorrow.[5]

Underhill learned how to find the elusive love so many never find. She heeded this first part of the answer Jesus gave the scribe who came seeking the single most important commandment by which to live. Jesus told him to go learn how to love God "with all his heart." Our striving for oneness of our heart with God should never cease.

Preparation

Those gathered will

- understand what it means to love God with the heart
- be equipped with ways to nourish love for the Divine in the human heart
- become aware of how what the heart loves affects life's balance

Key Questions

- Describe the current state of your heart. Does it have passion? imagination?
- Who or what has your heart and what does it need?
- Is your heart alive for God in any way? Does it inspire you to do anything for God?

Resources Needed

Newsprint and markers
Bibles
Paper and pencils or pens
The devotional song "Day by Day" for group singing (*optional*)

---

5. Dana Greene, *Evelyn Underhill: Artist of the Infinite Life* (New York: Crossroad Publishing Company, 1990), pp. 54–55.

Gathering

As the group gathers, divide into pairs (or threes if necessary) and read through the introduction to this session. Then reflect with each other on the following questions (or others you may have): What does it mean to give one's heart to God? How can we do this? Do you think this is an easy or difficult thing to do?

Balance Your Life

Look at the chart below. In column one, order the phrases according to the priority they have right now in the way you live in the heart of your life: one is lowest; ten is highest. In column two, reorder the list in the priority they would have if you were trying to order your life to unite your heart with God. What would rank high? What would rank low? What will change in you? Share your responses with other group members.

What I Love	Column 1	Column 2
Work		
Play		
Rest		
Nurturing my mind		
My social calendar		
My wardrobe		
My house and yard		
My time alone		
Sports		
Health and body		
Managing finances		
Family and core relationships		
Worship		
Service to the community		
Care for my spirit		

This chart is based on *Liberation of Life*, by Harvey and Lois Seifert (Nashville: The Upper Room, 1976), p. 24.

Exploring the Word

One person should read aloud Deut. 6:4–5. A second person should read aloud Mark 12:28–30. On newsprint write two sentences that are the focus for the session: "Hear, O Israel: The Lord is our God, the

Lord alone." (Deut. 6:4) and "[Y]ou shall love the Lord your God with all your heart" (Mark 12:30).

Take a minute or two in silence to contemplate the passages. Then discuss the following question: As you think about making God the one thing that matters for your life, how do you feel bodily and emotionally about the organization of your life right now? Become conscious of the tension that may be relieved and the balance that may be restored to you physically and mentally as you let go of all claims except this one claim on your live.

Develop an awareness of the power of the heart by discussing the symbols, images, and colors that have been used in history to describe or define the heart.

Discuss your answers and the following examples together. Read the Scriptures from Psalms and Ezekiel as you come to them:

1. What was in the heart of King Richard that made people call him "Lionhearted"?

_____

_____

_____

(*Answers:* Courage, determination, discipline, resolve.)

2. Read Ps. 39:2–3. What does the heart hold? Why does it need to belong to God?

_____

_____

_____

(*Answer:* The heart is the chamber where passion may live, desire may grow, and anger may fester.)

3. Read Ps. 139:23–24. What can the heart hide, and how can the heart's burdens be relieved?

_____

_____

_____

(*Answer:* The heart is a closet hiding what is deeply embedded in us, holding what may be broiling within us, or subconsciously working our true feelings out in our lives.)

4. Read Ezek. 36:26. How can the heart become a "stone" that needs to be restored to "flesh"?

_____

_____

5. Where have you seen the heart depicted as a pulsating, glowing, red organ? Why has it been pictured this way?

(*Answer:* It is a symbol of life and honored for emotional strength. It is depicted in folklore, in artwork, and in films.)

6. What clues do these examples offer for understanding how the heart can belong supremely to God?

Living the Word

It is one thing to take care of the heart because it is a major organ that affects the function of every other part of the body and the quality of our life. But it is another thing to understand it as the body's emotional seat with its own insight and perceptions. We are wise to pay more attention to this heart of ours. It can move the whole body or freeze it. It has much to do with what rules us, and what we try to rule. The heart then is a source of balance or imbalance for our lives. Jesus recommends we commit it to God.

Closing

A Prayer to Take with You

Lord, grant that I never shun the pain of giving birth to love, nor the fatigue of the effort that nurtures it from day to day. Teach me to value each moment as I value each beat of my own heart, and to find in the pulsing of my blood that distant tempo of birth, of growth, of love and of death which repeats itself over and over through a billion hearts and a million years, and which is the echo of the one eternal rhythm.[6]

---

6. Ernest Boyer, Jr., *A Way in the World: Family Life as Spiritual Discipline* (San Francisco: Harper & Row, 1984), p. 15.

　　　　　　　　　　　　　　　　　　　Life in Balance

The Spirited Life of the Soul

Scripture: Mark 12:30; Psalm 63:1–11

Introduction

"[Y]ou shall love the Lord your God with all your heart, and with all your soul . . . ." This, Jesus tells us, is the greatest commandment (Mark 12:30). But what differences exist between the heart and the soul? The two are often mentioned together, as if there is a brother-sister tie between them. Both are emotional human spheres; neither are of the material world. Both can animate the body or take the life away. Each has to do with what we desire; with what we long for, trust, and work to be closest to. Heart and soul always have an object or objects to adore. They also decide what we will abhor. They hold the eyes to what we will call beautiful.

In the Old Testament, the soul is not thought to be that part of us that is immortal, but the very life within us. The soul, like the heart, is the home of emotion and vitality.[1]

The Christian is the one who wants her or his soul to belong to God. When the scribe finds Jesus in the Gospel of Mark (12:28–30) and asks for the one commandment that could be called most beautiful, he may or may not have been trying to trap Jesus. There is no compelling reason in the text to think this was a tricky question rather than a search for some relief regarding all the laws and commandments the scribe was bound to accept and obey. In fact, scholars arguing for the authenticity of Mark's story note that a friendly scribe is unusual in the Gospels, and therefore, this story is probably true, for this one was friendly.[2] Whatever the case, all the demands of the law were a burden for this scribe; he and many others would surely welcome some rest for the soul.

As we look for ways to simplify and maintain balance in our lives against a world of demands and obligations that threaten to throw us

---

1. N. W. Porteous, "Soul," in *The Interpreter's Dictionary of the Bible*, edited by George A. Buttrick et al. (Nashville: Abingdon Press, 1984), p. 428.

2. Morna D. Hooker, *A Commentary on the Gospel According to St. Mark* (London: A&C Black, 1991), p. 286.

out of balance and distress us deep down in our souls, we will sense the soul's delight in the words Jesus spoke. There is great possibility in the pronouncement that was also Jesus' daily prayer: "Love the Lord your God . . . with all your soul." We may make it our own prayer and source of fortification.

Biblical Reflection

Plotinus defines ugly and beautiful for us, and the definitions have to do with who or what possesses our souls: "We possess beauty when we are true to our own being; ugliness is in going over to another order." He also describes the soul that has lapsed into belonging to what does not let it thrive: "Let the soul fall in with the Ugly," he says, "and at once it shrinks within itself, denies the thing, turns away from it, out of tune, resenting it"[3]

The soul is hard to capture and define, but from Scripture and experience we know that the soul can be beautiful or ugly, full or empty. It can be given to one or taken over by many. It can be a place of deep peace or great inner turmoil. Some describe a soul as being "lost" or "found." We say that our souls can soar, and they can fall. The human soul can be sound or sick and feel either hope or despair. But a soul fully alive is lovely by every human evaluation.

The soul is a mysterious part of us. It lets us know whether we are walking with God and refreshed as if by water or far away from where we belong, in some dry and thirsty land. A reading of Psalm 63 can bring all this to mind. The psalmist clearly knows and seeks a relationship with God that goes all the way to the soul. Here is one who is thirsty and hungry for God, who worships and prays. Whether the psalmist finds himself in the wilderness, with enemies, or in the temple, his relationship with God affects the essence of the state of his soul. God is his peace, when there is peace and when there is none. Clint McCann says this psalm "is fundamentally about life and its true source" since the word soul is used in verses 1, 5, and 8; life is used in verse 9; and they both connote vitality and even appetite.[4]

This one is obeying the great commandment. He is seeking God and only the things of God, such as truth. He already understands that those who divide themselves from the things that are not from God,

---

3. As quoted in *The Thought of the Heart and The Soul of the World*, by James Hillman (Dallas: Spring Publications, Inc., 1981), p. 59.

4. J. Clinton McCann, Jr., "The Book of Psalms," in *The New Interpreter's Bible* (Nashville: Abingdon Press, 1996), p. 927.

like lies, open their mouths to invite destruction and dissatisfaction into their souls.[5]

Please note that we are not told whether this way of reasoning and living saves this person's earthly life. Dr. James Mays says that in the days of the church fathers this psalm was given to those who valued God more than life and were even willing to become martyrs for what they believed about God.[6] We are not selling God as an amulet. The concern here is for the strength of the soul in the midst of strife.

Since God is one who keeps and restores the soul, the search for the balanced life is a search for ways to love God "with all [our] soul." This is a quest to be undivided by the many things that can ravage our souls. Life and stability come to us when the tremulous heart, the shaken souls, the boggled mind, and the sapped strength are centered in God. Often stress, illness, and anxiety get the best of us when we put our hearts and souls around something else.

We are invited to bring all of our "self" to live by and love one God when Jesus says, "You shall love the Lord your God with all your heart, and with all your soul, and with all your mind, and with all your strength" (Mark 12:30). It is an invitation to live in harmony rather than shifting in and out of balance.

Preparation

Those gathered will

- consider the differences and congruities between the heart and the soul
- discover what it means to love God with all your soul
- explore ways to replenish their souls and increase their devotion to God
- understand the balance in life that results from following Jesus' command

Key Questions

- What is your soul and how do you tend it?
- What one word describes the condition of your soul today?
- How much of God do you associate with your soul here and now, rather than after death?

---

5. Ibid., p. 928.
6. As quoted in ibid., p. 928.

- What is the relationship between your soul and the practice of your faith in your life?

Resources Needed

- Newsprint, tape, and markers
- Bibles
- Magazines and a few pairs of scissors

Gathering

To the leader: As the group members arrive, ask them to pick up a magazine and find some images that try to sell us the "good life." Ask them to look for ads that sell something that lifts the spirits or soothes the soul (herbs, drugs, foods and drink, hair tonic, etc.). Let participants share their selections and talk about the power and the delusion of each sales pitch.

Exploring the Word

Robert McAfee Brown says two things about spirituality that we should not forget: (1) spirituality includes liberation, and (2) the best definition for the spiritual life is "no more and no less than *following Jesus*."[7] His point is that loving God with all our heart and soul is more than slipping away to silent retreats and quiet places to be self-satisfied. It is much more than looking for sweet, personal peace and constant equilibrium in our own lives.

Those who love and regularly seek God with their souls are the ones who pray to keep a balanced perspective of this world. They want to make sure they see the sacred and the beautiful, in the place where heaven and hell both exist, and not simply keep the self alive and well-balanced.

The soul that is nourished by prayer and a sense of God is the soul that is kept by God and can be the soul that is stirred by God. Such a Spirit-filled soul can make a world of difference. Then the ears can hear and respond and the eyes can see—see the human struggle, the human joys, and the Creator's working hand—and both can offer to be a part of it all. God in our soul may mean the kind of peace that comes from challenging an injustice or taking a risk for the things of God. It is not simply a warm, individual feeling derived from soft words and a good night's sleep. The spiritual needs of our soul may be met when we see that a hungry child is fed.

7. Robert McAfee Brown, *Spirituality and Liberation: Overcoming the Great Fallacy* (Philadelphia: The Westminster Press, 1988), p. 117.

The love of God in our souls will increase our desire for such things. Jesus warned us about seeking after the peace of the world—it could leave us weary and void, and without a God-inspired soul at all.

- Read John 14:27. Discuss the life you seek as a Christian. What does *balance* really mean in this context?
- Meditate for a minute in silence on the second phrase in Mark 12:30.
- Pray aloud with other group members for one another's relationship with God.

Living the Word

The soul is all that enlivens you. It is the center of your longings. It controls the desires of your heart. The soul that loves God completely will need to be sustained by the spiritual practice of regular communion with God.

Examine your consciousness of God at work in your soul and how you nurture that awareness. Knowing that you can sense God in the ordinary as well as in the extraordinary, it is helpful to name the times, places, and ways you most powerfully experience God.

- When and where do you feel most alive and what are you doing? Does this experience belong to God? If not, how can it?
- Talk about a time when you felt lost or empty deep down in your soul. Can you name the reason why? Can you change the situation? How will you?
- Share your richest spiritual experience and describe its effect on your life. How will you continue to make it a part of your life?
- Name one way you could love God with your soul in a service-oriented or sacrificial way. Commit yourself to it, and let the group hold you accountable for it.
- Three times a day Jesus prayed to belong to God with all his heart, soul, and might. How often would you say you pray to love God with all your soul?

Closing

Contemplation is one more way for a soul to search for God. Contemplation opens the self up to receive God and experience the power of God's presence. In the time that remains, practice this contemplation exercise. In silence, focus on God and request from God a deeper relationship with God. Let your thoughts come and go, keeping your head clear. Relax and be still, feeling the soul seeking to be in touch with God. Ask only for one thing: a soul devoted to God. You may want to repeat a phrase to help you focus, such as "I have called you by name, you are mine" (Isa. 43:1).

You will need to do this often, daily, if your soul is to commune with God in trust and commitment. Watch for the change that will come to you.

Mindful of the Mind

Scripture: Mark 12:28–30; Luke 2:40; Philippians 1:9–11

Introduction

Everybody wants our minds. Teachers of all kinds want to guide it. Schools specializing in every field and a cadre of professionals are ready to train it. The media spends great sums of money to influence it, and the politicians work hard to win it. Family will shape it, and environment will fill it. Religion will vie for it, and a host of sources from the free world will sell information, send products, tout philosophies, and promote opinions until they believe they have bought it. But Jesus said God also wants the mind.

From time to time in the history of the church there have been those who propose that faith can work quite well with the heart and the soul but not with the mind. Their fear was that thinking too much would lead to faith's weakness—to doubt. They worried also that human knowledge (with its limited vision) and science (with its measuring tools and empirical facts) simply could not be compatible with the spiritual realm. The Enlightenment in particular was a time when science laughed at faith and faith denied science.

But we are encouraged to love God with all our mind and not be afraid of any discovery of truth. We are people who want to worship God "in spirit and truth" (John 4:24).

Therefore, when we allow faith to be strengthened by knowledge we are loving God with our minds. When we apply our minds to understanding the natural world and use its gifts for humanity's welfare out of our spiritual convictions that this is God's will, we serve God and fulfill our potential in God. And according to what Jesus said to the scribe, loving God with all our mind is not just a good idea, it is part of the one great command.

Biblical Reflection

"You shall love the Lord your God . . . with all your mind. . . ."
(Mark 12:28–30)

"The child [Jesus] grew and became strong, filled with wisdom; and the favor of God was upon him."

(Luke 2:40)

"And this is my prayer, that your love may overflow more and more with knowledge and full insight to help you to determine what is best, so that in the day of Christ you may be pure and blameless, having produced the harvest of righteousness that comes through Jesus Christ for the glory and praise of God."

(Phil. 1:9–11)

Once a man entered the land of fools. He saw everyone running from a field screaming, "There's a monster in the field!"

When he looked, he saw that their monster was a watermelon. He said to himself, "I'll teach these stupid people the difference between monsters and watermelon."

So he went into the field, picked up the watermelon, cut a piece out of it, and ate it. The people watched in astonishment. Then they ran to kill him shouting, "He's killed the monster and will kill us."

A few years later, another man entered the land of the fools and encountered a similar situation, only in this case he ran with them and lived among them. Aware that their monster was a watermelon, he slowly and gradually encouraged them to watch closely, and slowly he moved closer to it, thereby demonstrating that it was safe. Then one day the people discovered that the monster was really a fruit to eat and enjoy. Who, asks the Taoist, was the true teacher? The answer is, the one who let his life be a resource for the others' learning.[1]

Jesus spoke with the wisdom of the ages. He was a teacher to the teachers of wisdom, and he astounded many with his great knowledge and authority. But more than that, his life was the embodiment of wisdom. Jesus taught us how to think about God, ourselves, and others. He told us what to seek and how to live. Scripture does not record much about the childhood years of Jesus. But Luke's Gospel does take down the note that Jesus grew and trained in wisdom, fully devoting his whole mind to God: "The child [Jesus] grew and became strong, filled with wisdom; and the favor of God was upon him" (Luke 2:40).

---

1. John H. Westerhoff, *Spiritual Life: The Foundation for Preaching and Teaching* (Louisville: Westminster John Knox Press, 1994), pp. 44–45.

Life in Balance

With all his mind, in his wise words and ways, Jesus served God with all he had. And his life was held together in such single-minded devotion.

Paul prays for Christians in danger of being divided by their minds. New teachers are passing through offering the Philippians ways to live other than Christ's. Paul is concerned because torn minds lead to weakened spirits and broken community. He prays that they may be strong-minded, focused on God, and able to discern the truth. He prays that they will be able to know what love is and be strong-willed enough to give what it requires, so that love might flow more freely among them. He prays also for their ability to recognize what needs to be done and to have the insight to know how to accomplish it.[2]

Author Luke Timothy Johnson prepares us to commit ourselves to loving God with all our mind in five ways: with time, patience, suffering, faithfulness, and creativity. It will take time because learning does not occur any other way. It takes time to understand quantum physics and to understand the depths of love, and it will take time to comprehend the things of God.

It will ask for patience because learning is never easy. We will be called continually to trust as we journey toward God with the mind that wants to know when and why, and it will take alertness, a constant searching for God, if we expect to reach any new intellectual heights.

The effort to love God with the mind will include suffering because learning can often be painful. Opening up the mind wide enough to have more of the mysteries of God sit within is sure to stretch us, confound us, exhaust us, and at times discomfort us. What we discover of God may cause us to see the need to lose some things along the way. This too may hurt, but as the mind grows, we will have to grow up too.

The commitment to use the mind wholly to serve God will mean a commitment to being faithful to the promise of growing strong and stronger in our mind as long as we are able. This means neither wasting the mind nor taking the mind off God so that it can serve someone or something else. Jesus warned us that "no one can serve two masters" (Luke 16:13). To try to divide the mind to love God and something that is not about the things of God will be to abandon the love of God with all the mind.

And finally, the mind is the creative center of our being. As such, when it is fully given to the love of God, it is a pledge to serve God

---

2. Ralph P. Martin, *Philippians*. New Century Bible Commentary (Grand Rapids: Wm. B. Eerdmans Publishing Co., 1976), p. 68.

with imagination and energy. For the one who wants to live to please God, the mind cannot be spent on anything contradictory to God.[3] May our minds be dedicated and fully used for the glory of God.

Preparation

Those gathered will

- understand what it means to love God with the mind
- be encouraged to commit their minds to learn for the sake of serving God
- evaluate the level of devotion they give to God through the use of their minds

Key Questions

- What do you think the relationship between science and faith should be?
- How much time do you spend applying your mind to something that can be used to serve God? a week? a year?
- What could you do to use your mind more for the love and service of God?
- What would you have to change in order to do so?

Resources Needed

- Newsprint, tape, and markers
- Bibles
- Dictionary
- Paper and pencils or pens

Gathering

Play Fictionary

Have one person bring a dictionary to this session. Start by selecting one group member to go first. He or she selects an obscure word from the dictionary, tells the word (spelling it out if needed) to the rest of the group, and writes down the definition on a piece of paper. The other group members write down what they think the definition of the word could be. These can either be serious or humorous attempts at guessing the definitions. One person collects all the papers (including the one with the real definition) and reads all the "definitions" to the group. The group should then try to guess which definition is the real

---

3. Luke Timothy Johnson, *Living Jesus: Learning the Heart of the Gospel* (San Francisco: HarperSanFrancisco, 1999), p. 43.

one. Pass the dictionary to another person to select a word and begin again. Play two or three rounds.

Discussion

Read the introduction to this session and discuss with the entire group or in pairs the following questions: Who wants *your* mind? What does it mean to love God "with all your mind"?

Exploring the Word

It is painful to think of how the mind is bombarded in this age of information. We do our best to keep our minds focused on the things that matter. We check the boxes that guarantee us no more inundation of junk mail. We ask the customer service representatives not to call us with their offers, especially during dinner. But still we live in an age where the mind can barely keep up. We are the ones frantically clicking new keys and flipping through the "manuals for dummies"—trying to grow wise in a hurry. Often we are anxious and stressed by all these demands on our minds in this world of ours, where the machines, vocabulary, and rules are all new. Ask a ninety-year-old woman what a desktop or a notebook is and the twenty-year-old hearing her answer will snicker.

We are learning to accept the faster pace, but we are all searching for a way to slow down. Today our minds are threatened by overload, and we want protection, focus, and relief.

We could say we are a lot like that overprogrammed scribe who wanted Jesus to tell him which one thing he could remember and live to please God (Mark 12:28–30). In two sentences, which today might have been written on a small restickable adhesive paper, Jesus explained what was essential: "Hear O Israel: the Lord our God, the Lord is one; you shall love the Lord your God with all your heart, with all your soul, and with all your mind, and with all your strength" (Mark 12:29–30).

His command was not given to lay another responsibility on the mind, but to let the mind focus its strength and pour out its gifts only in the ways that bring glory to God.

Our Lord used his mind in great and powerful ways to show the wisdom of God. Often it was just the opposite of the wisdom of the world. Thus, loving God with our minds may not bring us earthly power or great success. This is no recipe for freedom from stress and migraines in a busy life either. It is a call to concentrate the mind on the things of God and tune out everything else. It is an exhortation to dedicate brain power only to things that God would approve, leaving everything else behind. We are welcomed to use all the strength of our minds to serve God alone.

Have someone read the following quote from Pascal slowly, so the words can be contemplated: "Submission and the use of reason; that is what makes true Christianity."[4]

Discuss the following questions: How does this quote support the study of the great commandment? How do we submit ourselves to God using our power of reason?

Living the Word

In an encyclical released in 1998, Pope John Paul II explained both the human need and hope for loving God with our minds: " 'Faith and reason,' " he said, " 'are like two wings on which the human spirit rises to the contemplation of the truth.' "[5] He wrote this to criticize our failure as Christians to help people think about the fundamental questions of life—such as "Who am I?" "Where did I come from?" and "Where am I going?"—so that they could be addressed honestly and openly before God. What do you think about this? Consider the following thought by Søren Kierkegaard and the commentaries by Diogenes Allen.[6] Share your response with the group.

> Another task or work of love is to take the trouble to learn what Christian love is, to see its uniqueness. Christian love has many imitations, and when one of these imitations is mistaken for Christian love, then God's love is not known.
>
> —Søren Kierkegaard

---

4. Pascal, as quoted in *Three Outsiders*, by Diogenes Allen (Cambridge, MA: Cowley Publications, 1983), p. 17.

5. Pope John Paul II, as quoted in *The Christian Century* (November 1998): 1086.

6. Allen, *Three Outsiders*, pp. 81–82.

Were Kierkegaard's point taken seriously, then perhaps we today might have been spared those bumper stickers which say, "Smile, God loves you." . . . For Kierkegaard any laziness in the use of our intellect, which should be used with all the power and discipline that can be mustered to understand and to articulate correctly what it is that God gives us, is a serious failure in our love. We are to use our minds in order to learn and speak rightly of Christian love, so that it may shine forth clearly, and by its light judge our lives and awaken in us a hunger for the glory of that perfection which is divine love.

—Diogenes Allen

What will you commit your mind to learn for the glory of God? Share your decision with the group and let them help you achieve your goal.

Closing

Have someone read aloud the following prayer of dedication: "Take, Lord, and receive all my liberty, my memory, my understanding, and my entire will, all that I have and possess. You have given all to me. To you, O Lord, I return it. All is Yours, dispose of it wholly according to your will. Give me your love and your grace, for this is sufficient for me."[6]

Note to the Leader: Look ahead to session 5 and be ready to have group members prepare and eat a meal together. If this is not feasible, perhaps you can all choose a restaurant to eat at for your next meeting.

6. Ignatius of Loyola, as quoted in *A Spiritual Formation Workbook: Small Group Resources for Nurturing Christian Growth,* by James Bryan Smith (San Francisco: HarperSanFrancisco, 1993), p. 13.

Devoting the Body Also to God

Scripture: Mark 12:28–30; Psalm 139:14; 1 Corinthians 6:12–13, 19–20

Introduction

It is fairly safe to say that Christians generally agree on these three principles:

1. Everything belongs to God.
2. We are to be good stewards of all that is in our care!
3. Words like waste, neglect, gluttony, and abuse belong in the category of sin and death, rather than salvation and life.

Oddly, few see how these Christian principles apply to the care for our own human bodies. In fact—with the exception of many sermons and admonitions about the evils and pitfalls of sex, drugs, and alcohol—Christianity has been much too silent about our responsibility for the body's health. In the great commandment, many have not paid much attention to loving God with all our strength and might.

But perhaps we are beginning a great awakening. Just recently I received an invitation from the pastoral care department of a hospital, offering me and other local ministers a weekend retreat. In itself that was an encouragement for the conscious care of my body. But in addition, the theme of the retreat was "taking care of ourselves while taking care of others," and the topics were physical health, mental health, and spirituality. There was even a guest speaker to discuss "a life of balance and harmony." The ideas were new, and yet they were old: "You shall love the Lord your God with all your heart, and with all your soul, and with all your mind, and with all your strength" (Mark 12:30).

Today the world is warming up to the idea of becoming more care-full of the body. We are discussing food labeling and nutrition, stressing the need for regular exercise, and finding ways to balance all the body's needs. It is no longer a concern for just athletes or the super body-conscious people; the quest for greater overall health and better living is widespread.

Some are beginning to recognize the ethical obligation for being more mindful of the body. They see the paradox of the great expectations we have for our bodies to carry us through years of wear, tear, and stress, while we give them such little maintenance. Others realize that we are paying high financial prices for our lack of bodily care and want to live more responsibly. Still others simply want to prolong youth, strength, vitality, and freedom of movement. They notice the consequences of ignoring the body and choose not to be forced to sit down earlier than they must or to suffer needlessly. And those who seek it as Christians find there is a long-standing theological basis for the care of the body: like the heart, the soul, and the spirit, the body also is to be dedicated to God and used for the glory of God.

The body is inseparably connected to the human spirit. We live in our earthly bodies as long as we live on this earth. They house our personalities and are our means for expressing, relating to others, and affecting our world. Thus, our attention to them is important. We do suffer consequences if the body is abused or left without proper care. We can see and feel the results of how we treat our bodies: how we eat and drink, how we work and rest, what we love, how we laugh and play, and how we suffer. Admittedly, we do not always get to choose everything we would like for the body, but goodness through the body comes from our faithful stewardship of it.

We are invited by Christ to allow every domain of human life to be brought into the spiritual realm and offered to God—from prayer and politics to sexuality and health.

Biblical Reflection

One of the scribes came near and heard them disputing with one another, and seeing that he answered them well, he asked him, "Which commandment is the first of all?" Jesus answered, "The first is, 'Hear, O Israel: the Lord our God, the Lord is one; you shall love the Lord your God with all your heart, and with all your soul, and with all your mind, and with all your strength.' "

(Mark 12:28–30)

"All things are lawful for me," but not all things are beneficial. "All things are lawful for me," but I will not be dominated by anything. "Food is meant for the stomach and the stomach for food," and God will destroy both one and the other. . . . Or do you not know that your body is a temple of the Holy Spirit within

you, which you have from God, and that you are not your own?
For you were bought with a price; therefore glorify God in your
body.

(1 Cor. 6:12–13a, 19–20)

"I praise you, for I am fearfully and wonderfully made. Wonderful
are your works; that I know very well."

(Ps. 139:14)

What does it mean to love God with all our strength? We understand
how to love God with our inner selves. We know to commit ourselves
to the discipline of prayer, worship, and service to others. We associate
the wellness of our hearts, the condition of our souls, and the training
of our minds with our spiritual lives. But loving God with our outer
strength has not been regarded as highly. We do not readily think of
our bodies as potential gifts to God.

Most have heard the church speak about the faithful stewardship of
our strength with regards to work. They have taught us that good work
is how we dedicate the strength of our bodies to God, and this is valid.
Making all our work pleasing to God is good. Both vocational choices
and earnings may be gifts to God. But we have limited this part of the
commandment and stopped short of thinking that the body itself can
glorify God.

Awareness of the mysteries and the marvels of the human body as a
part of God's creative power is enough to make the psalmist sing over
and over again (Psalm 119; 139). To notice that the body has strength
and beauty is to thank God for the gift and not neglect it: "I praise
you, for I am fearfully and wonderfully made. Wonderful are your
works; that I know very well" (Ps. 139:14).

Simply understanding that the body is made by God is enough to
warrant our good care for it. But instead we often push it and ignore it.
The human body is often wasted or overworked. It can be over- or
underfed. We can even fixate on our own bodies and pamper and
pump them to the point of idolatry. Either extreme hurts. Many are
hungering for ways to live better—in balance—through the body,
which affects one's whole being.

Unfortunately, we are susceptible to the attitude of the Corinthian
Christians who mistakenly held the view that "all things are lawful
[permissible] for me" (1 Cor. 6:12). This verse may be a general
"freedom statement" that Paul himself made earlier to followers of

Christ. If it is, the Corinthians are abusing it. They have taken it to the extreme so that now Paul needs to write to them and qualify and define "freedom in Christ" with specific issues like food and sexuality. Other interpreters suggest that "freedom in Christ" is the Corinthians' current motto and mind-set. Paul is writing to argue against it in a point-counterpoint manner.[1] Either way, the conversation is stark.

For Paul, "freedom in Christ" is not some cheap phrase. It has been hard won in the body of Christ. Paul shows us by his life that freedom is choosing what is best in the eyes of God rather than choosing what is the personal pleasure of the moment that leads us toward self-inflicted enslavement and death. Our life comes from living for the glory of God.[2]

The Shema challenges us to think differently. Jesus tells us to pray daily for the ability to give consciously everything in our power and under our care to God, including our bodies. Quoting the Shema in the Gospel of Mark (Mark 12:28–30), Jesus asks us to love and serve God with everything we are, as creatures with a heart and a soul, with a mind, and with physical strength.

It may be time to feel a new solidarity between the body and the soul and to choose today to live a more disciplined, dedicated life. At the moment, where have your choices led you?

Preparation

Those gathered will

- consider the care of the body as stewardship
- decide in concrete ways how to balance and enhance life through the body
- explore ways to dedicate the body to greater life and the glory of God

Key Questions

- What effect does our current social environment have on the body and what might some of our short-term pleasures do to our long-term well-being?
- How can the body be given to God?
- How true is the saying "You are what you eat"?

---

1. Elizabeth Schüssler Fiorenza, "1 Corinthians," in *Harper's Bible Commentary*, edited by James L. Mays et al. (San Francisco: Harper & Row, 1998), p. 1176.

2. Marion L. Soards, "First Corinthians," in *Mercer Commentary on the Bible*, edited by Watson E. Mills and Richard F. Wilson et al. (Macon, GA: Mercer University Press, 1995), pp. 1172–73.

- What goals can be made for increasing awareness of your body as a spiritual matter between God and you?
- How can you increase your body's strength and give that to God?

Resources Needed

- Newsprint, markers, and tape
- Bibles
- Food for putting together a healthy meal and time to enjoy eating together
- Menus with healthy choices to share

Working Together

You will be preparing and eating a meal together this session (unless you choose to go to a restaurant). Have fun with it! Laugh together as you share in the meal preparation! Make sure you divide up tasks ahead of time. Who's bringing what? Whose house/apartment will this be at? And, most important, who's doing the dishes? (Be sure not to leave your host with a sinkful of dirty pots and pans!) And be sure to have a healthy menu, taking into account any food allergies or preferences people might have.

Gathering

Just for fun

As you begin to prepare the meal, test yourselves on the following classifications of eating.[3] Give points for each correct answer. Laugh a little. You may want to reward the winner with a healthy treat.

Lacto—one who eats dairy

Ovo—one who eats eggs

Ovo-lacto—one who eats eggs and dairy

Pesca—one who eats fish

Involuntary Vegetarian—one who eats plant food because everyone around him or her does and there's simply no other choice.

Primary Color Vegetarian—one who eats some red meat once in a blue moon.

Fast-food Eater—one who eats whatever can be grabbed as quickly as possible with no regard to the needs of the body beyond the immediate cessation of hunger and pleasure of the tongue.

The Heart Attacker—one who eats the following foods until he or she is more than full: Breakfast: three eggs, fried in butter; six pieces of bacon

---

3. Donna Sapolin, "Of Cheese and Chocolate," *Vegetarian Times* (February 1999): 5.

and sausage; hash browns, cooked in lard; bread toasted, buttered, and jellied. Lunch: bologna and cheese on white bread smothered with mayo; liter of soda; bag of potato chips, and four to six cookies. Dinner: thick T-bone steak; mound of french fries with cheese; chocolate cake with two scoops of ice cream.[4]

Exploring the Word

Approximately 2600 Americans die each day from cardiovascular disease. That is one death each thirty-three seconds.[5] Our life is about a body and a spirit. Both are valuable and both need care. The Old Testament thinks of human beings in terms of "flesh" and "soul."[6] It takes a holistic approach that sees no way to divide the personality or the spirit from the flesh. We are *nephesh*, "a living being" (Gen. 2:7), and the physical is acknowledged in conjunction with the spiritual. In this understanding, human beings are filled with life and are potentially active only when soul and flesh work together.[7]

In the ancient Greek world, this was not the case. The soul was the only concern. The soul was supreme. It alone was "heavenly" and "spiritually higher" than the body. On the other hand, Plato called the body a "tomb." Sadly, he viewed it as a plague on humans, a prison we must endure for awhile, rather than as a gift from God. He saw it less as something for experiencing human relationships and God's world than as something fashioned from earth's dust for human functioning while on earth only. Thus the body was not regarded in that society as part of the "self" that mattered. It was tied to the earth, merely an object of corruption, and the ancient Greeks deemed it unholy. Therefore God cared nothing about it either, they reasoned.

Yet for Christians, the body is much more valuable. In the New Testament Jesus takes time to touch people and heal the body (Mark 5:29). The disciples are encouraged to watch over their bodies sexually and emotionally, to keep them free from adultery (Matt. 5:29), from anxiety (Matt. 6:25), and from fear (Matt. 10:28) for the sake of God's glory and their wholeness. Paul asks us to give our bodies to God's service and glory (Rom. 12:1). He disciplines his body so that he

---

4. Ronni Sandroff, "The Heart of the Matter," *Vegetarian Times*, p. 77.

5. *1998 Heart and Stroke Statistical Update*, (Washington, DC: American Heart Association, 1998), p. 3.

6. R. Eduard Schweizer, "Body," in *The Anchor Bible Dictionary*, vol. 1, edited by David Noel Freedman, et al. (New York: Doubleday, 1992), p. 768.

7. Thomas H. Troeger, *Meditation: Escape to Reality* (Philadelphia: The Westminster Press, 1977), p. 34.

might better serve God (1 Cor. 9:27) and talks about how this makes him free. He reminds us that the body matters; it is the temple of the Holy Spirit (1 Cor. 6:19–20), and in the end, Paul believes we will be accountable to God for what we have done "in the body" (2 Cor. 5:10).

Clearly, the body may be neglected and even scorned. Or it may be celebrated, embraced, and given to God with love, dedication, and care.

Stewardship of Our Bodies

On a scale of one to five, how do you rate yourself on the stewardship of your body? on living a balanced life?

	1	2	3	4	5
Exercise					
Rest					
Food					
Work					
Play					
Worry					
Laughter					
Solitude					
Prayer					
Meditation					
Relationships					
Human touch					
Community					

Discuss with one another ways to balance your lives, simplify them, enrich them, and take your bodies' human needs more seriously.

Living the Word

All of us may glorify God with the strength we have been given. But some have more strength than others. A person who is aged, terminally ill, mentally challenged, or permanently disabled has limitations and extra hardships, but we are all equally encouraged to seek our greatest potential for bodily wellness as long as we have one to tend.

At the same time, it is important to name the difference between serving God with our physical strength and serving ourselves by it. There is always the temptation to turn anything into self-glorification. When this happens with the body, we turn all focus in on ourselves. When we become obsessive about muscles and food, the perfect poundage and form, and how we look, life's balance is lost and Jesus' prayer is perverted.

God save us from the person who spends hours a day conditioning and perfecting the body, desiring to become a shining example of health for the world to admire, and wearing the T-shirt with the great commandment emblazoned across a bulging chest. This is not the point. God is not served.

Discuss together:

- How are physical health and spiritual health related in our world?
- Where do you draw the line between the body and God?

Case Studies

Read the following case studies and comments. Discuss in pairs or as a whole group the questions that follow each case study.

Case Study One: For or Against the Body—Sex

"We are sexual beings and our sexuality does affect our spiritual wellbeing."[8] In the Hebrew Bible, *yada* means knowing another person as a complete and whole human being. That means going deeper than "a quickie or an affair or a short-term relationship would allow." Sex affects the personality. It touches the human psyche.[9]

- In our society, do current expressions of human sexuality seem healthy? Are they pleasing to God?
- How aware do you think we are of the inseparable nature of the body with the mind and the soul?

Case Study Two: Habits That Hurt; Habits That Help

Hurt: "I feel stressed out, tired, and pent-up. I'm out of balance." "I drink lots of coffee, skip meals, and work so that I don't see the light of day." "I eat fast-food in my car and keep sugar at my desk. There's no time to care for my body; I don't get much sleep. I can't even find five minutes to breathe."

Help: "One of my primary ways to nourish everything—body, mind, and spirit—is to go for a walk first thing in the morning. It gets the juices flowing not only physically but in terms of praying and writing poetry. Often I pray as I walk, especially if I've got particular people I'm

8. Richard J. Foster, *Richard J. Foster's Study Guide to the Challenge of the Disciplined Life* (San Francisco: Harper & Row, 1985), p. 4.

9. Leonard Felder, "The Decalogue: Commandments or Challenges?" *Word & World* 18, no. 1 (Winter 1988): 67.

concerned about. I think the steady rhythm of walking is conducive to letting the mind wander in very good ways."[10]

- Ask yourselves why you treat your body the way you do. Name the cause. Is it due to stress, anxiety, emotional discomfort, habits, addictions, your schedule, or lack of awareness? Discuss ways to live better.
- Share some good choices you can make from typical menus at restaurants. Agree to select a meal that is respectful of the body, adds to quality of life, and may even help keep future national health-care costs at a minimum.
- Brainstorm together about how to find or make time for yourself. Consider a one-day retreat, a day off from cooking or car pooling, one morning a week to sleep in, one afternoon to take a long walk. Honor God and yourself this way.

Closing

End your meal or time together with the following charge and benediction, or have someone from your group close with prayer: "May the God of peace himself sanctify you entirely; and may your spirit and soul and body be kept sound and blameless at the coming of our Lord Jesus Christ. The one who calls you is faithful, and he will do this" (1 Thess. 5:22–24).

---

10. Kathleen Norris, as quoted in Lynn Garrett, "12 Ways to Raise Your Spirits," *Fitness Magazine* (April 1988): 72.

The Strength of Our Days

Scripture: Mark 12:28–30; Romans 6:12–14

Introduction

An encounter with the living God does something to us. God shows us what is good, and we are not the same as we were before. We have new eyes to see. Now the mind focuses on what might be, and the spirit is energized by the hope of reaching the goal. The heart now desires, and so we live and move in new strength toward the prize, until we have gained what pleases God and gives us joy.

To experience God, then, is to be called to something totally—in heart, soul, mind, and strength. We are made ready to live in deeper moments with God, in more fulfilling days with others. Our opened eyes want to see more clearly, and we run with greater deft after the things God has taught us to choose. When this happens to us, we will pursue the love of God in every way, with all we are, without growing weary or faint (Isa. 40:31). When we meet God and agree to follow after the example of Christ, we go on in new strength, maturing all along the way, until God grants us our peace and fulfillment.

Someone on a quest for spiritual meaning answered a survey about the subject. Observing the Spirit of God moving in the lives of others, he wrote:

> As I watch people in the maturing process, I discover that those individuals who have a close and personal relationship with Jesus Christ as their Savior and Lord in their life exhibit maturity in a way which others do not. This is particularly true of young people who often mature "overnight" as they come into a new relationship with Jesus Christ and as they find purpose and a center to their thought process and their entire being.[1]

In today's world, images of mature people are rare and highly sought after, particularly those whose entire selves are centered in purpose and

---

1. Charles C. L. Kao, "Christian Maturity in Psychosocial Perspective," in *Maturity and the Quest for Spiritual Meaning*, edited by Charles C. L. Kao (Lanham, MD: University Press of America, 1988), p. 13.

meaning. Those who are confident in what they do, who they are, and what they believe are greatly admired, especially when there is a strange peace all about them, keeping them calm in a whirlwind of option, opinion, and activity. We are a population in search of such direction. We all look for the God who calms storms and directs lives. Sometimes we look in thousands of places. But for the Christian community there is one God making one call to us. For us to hear that call and respond to it is the hope of God.

The claim is that life with God—dedicating all we have and hold to God—leads us to the surest foundation on which to build the "whole" life human beings so desire. But be ready to defend this way if you take it, because the world does not always agree that a commitment to God is an orientation toward life, balance, wholeness, and health. After all, our symbol is a cross, and it means loss, pain, sacrifice, and death. We do not offer Christian faith as a health remedy. We gather for grace and peace, but we struggle through conflict and live to give ourselves away too. Despite newspaper reports, this way is not about gaining a health advantage from sitting in a church pew and loving God.[2]

We do not guarantee anyone the sweetest life or extra years from being faithful, as if God is a self-help cocktail you swallow in order to slip into the good life. The call to love God with all your heart, soul, mind, and strength is to begin to think harder about a deeper commitment to God in the trust that a life lived for God is a good life.

Biblical Reflection

One of the scribes came near and heard them disputing with one another, and seeing that he answered them well, he asked him, "Which commandment is the first of all?" Jesus answered, "The first is, 'Hear, O Israel: the Lord our God, the Lord is one; you shall love the Lord your God with all your heart, and with all your soul, and with all your mind, and with all your strength.' "

(Mark 12:28–30)

Therefore, do not let sin exercise dominion in your mortal bodies, to make you obey their passions. No longer present your members to sin as instruments of wickedness, but present yourselves to God as those who have been brought from death to life; and present your members to God as instruments of righteousness. For sin

2. Frederick J. Gaiser, "Is Spirituality Good for You?" *Word and World* (Winter 1998): p. 3.

will have no dominion over you, since you are not under law but under grace.

(Rom. 6:12–14)

To say the least, Jesus' words are thorough. The human commitment to God begins in the center and reaches from head to toe. It covers inside and out. It asks for us to love God with all our heart, soul, mind, and strength. There is nothing left for anyone or anything else to have—or take—before God gets us first.

What is interesting is how God's taking is really God's giving. The offer is this: Do you want an undivided life for a change? Would you like one voice to answer to for everything? Do you want to build your life on a single foundation, instead of a thousand? Life by this commandment calms the frenzied world. It can put everything else into perspective for a lifetime—all is under God's eye and in God's care. This is not the easy way; but this is peace and good purpose.

Theologically the Shema means that God is the only power to rely on. God is the center where we long to be; God is the ground of being that undergirds all there is that is of value and meaning in life. The statement in essence says we are unable to be whole or find what is meaningful any time we stray from this source of being.

This word to us, the Shema, is deeply personal and pastoral. It is a plea from God for us to choose God. It is a hope that we will base our life on what is not chaotic, illusionary, or duplicitous. It is an invitation, an urgent one, for us to know what makes human life good and to choose it. The demand of the Shema "is ultimately the gift of grace."[3]

I am thankful Paul sympathizes with us as we try to follow the demands of the Shema. The book of Romans tells the redundant story of our human struggle in a paragraph. First, we agree to see that our passions do not rule us; of course, we want nothing that will hurt us to have dominion over us. Yes, we will resist any evil controlling our hearts or minds. Naturally, we want to choose life rather than death and to continue in it wholeheartedly. But even Paul, who pummels his body for the sake of Christ (Rom. 7:14–15) experiences the frustration we commonly experience every time we make and break resolutions. We "will" to do something but do not do it. We agree on what is healthy and highly recommended but fail to live up to it.

---

3. Patrick D. Miller, *Deuteronomy*. Interpretation: A Bible Commentary for Teaching and Preaching (Louisville: John Knox Press, 1990), pp. 103–104.

There is a reason for our warfare. Human passions and desires can be swayed, and the seat of our will is movable—so we are often self-divided and led away from where we really want to be. Sin is what we call this power that persuades us to do what we say we do not want to do. The power of sin tempts us away from loving God with "all our heart, soul, mind, and strength" and pulls us from our center with God over and over again.

Since human beings are not spirit *or* flesh, but spirit *and* flesh, we sin inevitably. We exist with strengths and weaknesses all at the same time. We are both bound to sin and freed from it for a lifetime. We will always know sweet victory and agonizing defeat in the human psyche. This is not a moral dilemma we face, but a state of being.[4]

But we live under grace. Therefore we are not people who live without hope of being able to present our total selves before God or choose well. Our hope is in Christ, who knew how to obey God alone and forgives us when we flounder and fail. Our strength is in Christ, who broke the power of sin and was granted life rather than death.

The hope of Christ's constancy with God is our inspiration. When the searching scribe came asking about what really matters, Jesus told him to love God with consistent and total devotion, perfectly, and with all his being—heart, soul, mind, and strength.

This awareness of our call—to let only God control us—is the motivation for every action and use of our life, and perceiving our real ability to resist sin, with God's help, is what keeps us from ever giving up. It is our vantage ground. The same Spirit of God that kept Christ may now dwell in and guard us.

We may find new eyes to see what destruction is and avoid it. Now we may have more than human will power and herbs! We are privileged with renewable strength—to strive again and again to live past all that contradicts wholeness and the will of God. Now we, too, might move more steadily from death to life, rather than back and forth, in and out of balance, or even in reverse.

With God, new life is always possible. Changes can be made in the heart, in the soul, in the mind, and in the body. In the Christian life there is strength for our days. Thanks be to God!

---

4. Paul Achtemeier, *Romans* (Atlanta: John Knox Press, 1985), p. 122.

Preparation

Those gathered will

- explore the advantage of having one authority and one story for the rule of their lives
- clarify who they are and who they want to be
- better understand the human struggle to be whole and contented

Key Questions

- How balanced is your life in relationship with God? with others? with yourself?
- What are we up against in today's world? How will we find our way to wholeness and balance in life?

Resources Needed

- Magazines
- Scissors and markers
- Glue
- Newsprint or poster board
- Self-assessment inventory (found on p. 46)

Gathering

As you arrive read the introduction and biblical reflection sections at the beginning of this session. Then complete the inventory describing who you feel you are today.[5]

In column A use the number scale to indicate how you feel now: 5 = very true; 4 = often true; 3 = sometimes true; 2 = occasionally true; 1 = not true. In column B put a plus if you would like to increase that feeling or attribute or a minus if you would like to lessen it.

Then select five items you now most strongly want to change and mark those answers. Share with the group or simply ask them to pray for your success in the future.

---

5. Adapted from Jackie M. Smith, *Leading Groups in Personal Growth* (Richmond, VA: John Knox Press, 1973), pp. 108–110.

	A	B
1. I fear failure in anything I want to accomplish.	___	___
2. I am contented.	___	___
3. I am relaxed.	___	___
4. I am no one.	___	___
5. I am a person with something to give.	___	___
6. I usually like people.	___	___
7. I am a responsible person.	___	___
8. I am aware of being somewhat at cross-purposes with myself.	___	___
9. I am often emotionally impulsive.	___	___
10. I give in easily.	___	___
11. I long for deeper relationships.	___	___
12. I do not feel very valuable.	___	___
13. I have trouble facing the truth about myself.	___	___
14. I often feel helpless.	___	___
15. I am open and honest with others and myself.	___	___
16. I am using most of my gifts and talents.	___	___
17. I feel I am sexually attractive.	___	___
18. I feel apathetic.	___	___
19. I have a healthy love for myself.	___	___
20. I feel guilty about too many things.	___	___
21. I am often anxious.	___	___
22. I keep worrying about my health.	___	___
23. I really enjoy life.	___	___
24. I feel wholehearted in my actions and at one with myself.	___	___
25. I have good friends.	___	___
26. I feel adequate.	___	___
27. I am sensitive and responsive to others.	___	___
28. I find it easy to forgive others.	___	___
29. I am easily hurt by others.	___	___
30. I feel pulled in too many directions.	___	___
31. I am afraid of conflict.	___	___

Exploring the Word

Today's postmodern world is a quickly changing, curiously open-ended world much like the eccentric one portrayed in *Alice in Wonderland*, where there are rabbits to chase, paths to explore, adventures to take, and plenty of things that say, "Try Me." In the end, Alice sits down and cries from all her confusion and lostness.

We are wisdom-, truth-, and meaning-seekers, trying out a spirituality smorgasbord in a theological vacuum. Visiting cathedrals and chapels, we might also go from bookshop to workshop to spiritual guides. We might try poetry from the mystics of old or music from the New Age, Celtic or Gregorian Chant traditions. We might listen to a little Eastern philosophy, some medieval wisdom, or pop psychology for daily inspiration; or we may try to find comfort in pharmaceuticals, homeopathic medicines, and other promising rituals.

Christians do not look with great disdain and total skepticism on all this. We are not looking to be closed-minded isolationists. We do not aim to be automatically suspicious of change and choice. But we are a people with a story.

When we try to understand things like life and death, maturity and aging, forgiveness and freedom, sickness and health, fear and peace, family and society, we trust in the eternal truths and the authority of God. Our hearts, souls, minds, and strength are set on the teachings of Christ. We are those who hear the voice of God and choose to follow it. We have a story of faithfulness and devotion and a ground of being that will not let our lives be carried and controlled by legions. We are committed to one—God. Our daily prayer is the prayer Jesus' prayed from childhood on, the Shema. We will "love the Lord our God, and with all our heart, and with all our soul, and with all our mind, and with all our strength."

Living the Word

Human beings have a need to be in balance. We need a life with rhythm and flow. We need to know how to work and play, when to be alone and in community with others, and how to choose life and keep ourselves close to God, our maker. We may need to simplify our lives and contemplate the fresh and peaceful idea of serving one, of serving God alone. Or we may need to change direction or refocus our lives so that we live in greater harmony with God, others, and ourselves.

May God grant us the grace to walk with God in body, in mind, and in spirit. May we grow into a spiritual life that is strong through our joys and sufferings, holding on to God's command, knowing what it is for us: power, fullness, and freedom.

Self-Portraits

On one side of a piece of newsprint or poster board, ask group members to express the many desires, pressures, and conflicts they see now in their lives—both their inner and outer selves.

On the other side of the paper, show how they envision themselves as God is calling them to be.[6]

Have members discuss their portraits and their hopes for the future.

Closing

End your time together by sharing memories of the past few weeks: what you have learned about each other, what you have learned about yourselves, and what if anything you plan to change in your life as a result of this study.

Make a pact as a group to continue meeting, either to continue more Bible study or to see one another on an informal, social basis. Better yet, do both!

End with the following prayer, or one of your own:

I pray that, according to the riches of his glory, he may grant that you may be strengthened in your inner being with power through his Spirit, and that Christ may dwell in your hearts through faith, as you are being rooted and grounded in love. I pray that you may have the power to comprehend, with all the saints, what is the breadth and length and height and depth, and to know the love of Christ that surpasses knowledge, so that you may be filled with all the fullness of God. Now to him who by the power at work within us is able to accomplish abundantly far more than all we can ask or imagine, to him be glory in the church and in Christ Jesus to all generations, forever and ever. Amen.

(Eph. 3:16–21)

---

6. Ibid., p. 39.

For Further Study

Confessions, by Augustine.

Care of the Soul: A Guide for Cultivating Depth and Sacredness in Everyday Life, by Thomas Moore. New York: Harper Collins, 1992.

Dramatic Pauses: 20 Ready-to-Use Sketches for Youth Ministry, by Jim Hancock. Grand Rapids: Zondervan Publishing House, 1995.

Erudition at God's Service, edited by John R. Sommerfeldt. Kalamazoo, MI: Cistercian Publications, 1987.

FamilyFun's Games on the Go, edited by Lisa Stiepock. New York: Hyperion, 1998.

Habits of the Heart, by Robert Bellah. San Francisco: Harper & Row, 1985.

Full Catastrophe Living: Using the Wisdom of Your Body and Mind to Face Stress, Pain, and Illness, by Jon Kabat-Zinn. New York: Dell, 1990.

The Marriage Journey: Preparations and Provisions for Life Together, by Linda Grenz and Delbert C. Glover. Boston: Cowley Publications, 1996.

Plain Prayers in a Complicated World, by Avery Brooke. Boston: Cowley Publications, 1993.

Seeds of the Spirit: Wisdom of the Twentieth Century, edited by Richard H. Bell with Barbara L. Battin. Louisville: Westminster John Knox Press, 1995.

Soul Feast: An Invitation to the Christian Spiritual Life, by Marjorie Thompson. Louisville: Westminster John Knox Press, 1995.

The Soul of Sex: Cultivating Life as an Act of Love, by Thomas Moore. New York: Harper Collins, 1988.

Spirit Windows: A Handbook of Spiritual Growth Resources for Leaders, by Ann Z. Kulp. Louisville: Bridge Resources, 1998.

Tuesdays with Morrie: An Old Man, A Young Man, and Life's Greatest Lesson, by Mitch Albom. New York: Doubleday Publishing, 1997.

Worry: Controlling It and Using It Wisely, by Edward M. Hallowell. Canada: Random House Audiobooks, 1997.

For more information on health-related issues, check www.healthline.com.

Bibliography

Achtemeier, Paul. *Romans*. Atlanta: John Knox Press, 1985.

Allen, Diogenes. *Three Outsiders*. Cambridge, MA: Cowley Publications, 1983.

Boyer, Ernest, Jr. *A Way in the World: Family Life as Spiritual Discipline*. San Francisco: Harper & Row, 1984.

Brown, Robert McAfee. *Spirituality and Liberation: Overcoming the Great Fallacy*. Philadelphia: The Westminster Press, 1988.

Craigie, Peter C. *The Book of Deuteronomy*. Grand Rapids: Wm. B. Eerdmans, 1976.

Dawn, Marva J. "Pop Spirituality or Genuine Story?" *Word & World* 18, no. 1 (Winter 1998): 48.

De Mello, Anthony. *One Minute Wisdom*. New York: Doubleday & Company, Inc., 1986.

Felder, Leonard. "The Decalogue: Commandments or Challenge?" *Word & World* 18, no. 1 (Winter 1998): 67.

Fiorenza, Elizabeth Schüssler. "1 Corinthians." In *Harper's Bible Commentary*, edited by James L. Mays, et al. San Francisco: Harper & Row, 1988.

Foster, Richard J. *Richard J. Foster's Study Guide to the Challenge of the Disciplined Life*. San Francisco: Harper & Row, 1985.

Gaiser, Frederick J. "Is Spirituality Good for You?" *Word & World* 18, no. 1 (Winter 1998): 3.

Garrett, Lynn. "12 Ways to Raise Your Spirits." *Fitness Magazine* (April 1998): 72.

Greene, Dana. *Evelyn Underhill: Artist of the Infinite Life*. New York: Crossroad Publishing Company, 1990.

Hillman, James. *The Thought of the Heart and The Soul of the World*. Dallas: Spring Publications, Inc., 1981.

Hooker, Morna D. *A Commentary on the Gospel According to St. Mark*. London: A&C Black, 1991.

Johnson, Luke Timothy. *Living Jesus: Learning the Heart of the Gospel.* San Francisco: HarperSanFrancisco, 1999.

Kao, Charles C. L., ed. *Maturity and the Quest for Spiritual Meaning.* London: University Press of America, 1988.

Mann, Thomas, W. *Deuteronomy.* Westminster Bible Companion. Louisville: Westminster John Knox Press, 1995.

Martin, Ralph P. *Philippians.* New Century Bible Commentary. Grand Rapids: Wm. B. Eerdmans Publishing Co., 1976.

McCann, J. Clinton, Jr. "The Book of Psalms," in *The New Interpreter's Bible.* Nashville: Abingdon Press, 1996.

McClellan, Keith. *Prayer Therapy.* St. Meinrad, IN: Abbey Press, 1990.

Miller, Patrick D. *Deuteronomy.* Interpretation: A Bible Commentary for Teaching and Preaching. Louisville: John Knox Press, 1990.

Peck, M. Scott. *The Road Less Traveled: A New Psychology of Love, Traditional Values, and Spiritual Growth.* New York: Simon & Schuster, 1978.

Porteous, N. W. "Soul." In *The Interpreter's Dictionary of the Bible*, edited by George A. Buttrick et al. Nashville: Abingdon Press, 1984.

Sandroff, Ronni. "The Heart of the Matter." *Vegetarian Times* (February 1999): 77.

Sapolin, Donna. "Of Cheese and Chocolate." *Vegetarian Times* (February 1999): 5.

Schweizer, Eduard R. "The Body." In *The Anchor Bible Dictionary*, vol. 1, edited by David Noel Freedman, et al. New York: Doubleday, 1992.

Seifert, Lois and Harvey. *Liberation of Life: Growth Exercises in Meditation and Action.* Nashville: The Upper Room, 1976.

Smith, Jackie M. *Leading Groups in Personal Growth.* Richmond, VA: John Knox Press.

Smith, James Bryant. *A Spiritual Formation Workbook: Small Group Resources for Nurturing Christian Growth.* San Francisco: HarperSanFrancisco, 1989.

Soards, Marion L. "First Corinthians." In *Mercer Commentary on the Bible*, edited by Watson E. Mills, Richard F. Wilson et al. Macon, GA: Mercer University Press, 1995.

Troeger, Thomas H. *Meditation: Escape to Reality*. Philadelphia: The Westminster Press, 1977.

Von Rad, Gerhard. *Deuteronomy: A Commentary*. The Old Testament Library. Philadelphia: The Westminster Press, 1966.

Westerhoff, John. *Spiritual Life: The Foundation for Preaching and Teaching*. Louisville: Westminster John Knox Press, 1994.

Wicks, Robert J. *Seeking Perspective: Weaving Spirituality and Psychology in Search of Clarity*. New York: Paulist Press, 1991.

About the Author

 Page L. D. Creach is a Minister of the Word and Sacrament of the Presbyterian Church (U.S.A.). She has served as pastor to congregations in Virginia and North Carolina and currently is Associate Minister to First Presbyterian Church in Rocky Mount, North Carolina. She is married to Jerome F. D. Creach, a professor of biblical studies, writer, teacher, and minister in the Presbyterian Church (U.S.A.). They have one daughter, Adair, who also loves the church.